W9-API-843

BIRD WATCHING for KIDS

A FAMILY BIRD WATCHING GUIDE

By Steven A. & Elizabeth May Griffin

The Outdoor Kids Series

FROM

NORTHWORD
PRESS, INC

MINOCQUA, WISCONSIN

© Steven A. and Elizabeth May Griffin, 1995

All rights reserved. No part of this book may be reproduced or transmitted in any form or copied by any means, electronic or mechanical, without written permission of the publisher. Copyrights on all photographs contained herein are the property of the photographer. No photographs in this book may be reproduced in any form without the express written consent of the photographer.

Cover design by Russell S. Kuepper
Other design by Amy J. Monday

Published by: NorthWord Press, Inc.
            P.O. Box 1360
            Minocqua, WI 54548

For a free catalog describing NorthWord's line of books and gift items,
call toll free 1-800-336-5666

Printed in U.S.A.

Library of Congress Cataloging-in-Publication Data

Griffin, Steven A.
    Bird watching for kids / by Steven A. Griffin & Elizabeth May Griffin.
        p.   cm. -- (Outdoor kids)
    Includes index.
    ISBN 1-55971-457-3
    1. Bird watching--Juvenile literature. [1. Bird watching.
2. Birds.] I. Griffin, Elizabeth May. II. Title.
III. Series: Outdoor kids series.
    QL677.5.G76 1995
    598'.07234--dc20   94-40013
                                            CIP
                                            AC

Opposite page: Robin.

Acknowledgments

The authors wish to thank Howard Griffin, Mary Jo Griffin,
Gary Haske, and especially our favorite librarian, Cheryl Levy,
for reading the manuscript and offering helpful tips—
for which the reader may also be thankful.

Photography by:

© 1994 Richard Hamilton Smith, 3, 48, 56, 82.
© 1994 Dembinsky Photo Associates, 12, 14, 21, 23, 31, 39,
        45, 52, 62, 66 (top left & right, bottom right) 77, 78, 79.
© 1994 Tom and Pat Leeson, 28, 37, 61, 74.
© 1994 Tom Stack and Associates, 8, 10, 32, 34, 43, 47, 60,
        64, 66 (lower left), 69, 70, 72, 80, 86.
© 1994 The Wildlife Collection, 44, 73.
© 1994 Steven A. Griffin, 24, 26, 50, 54.
© 1994 Photobank, Inc., 53.
© 1994 Lawrence A. Michael, 58.
© 1994 Bruce Coleman, Inc., 68.
© 1994 John Netherton, 16, 40, 84.
© 1994 Gregory K. Scott, 18, 51.
© 1994 Martha McBride/Unicorn Stock Photos, Cover.

Dedication

This book is dedicated to Elizabeth's grandparents,
Theresa Yob and Howard and Margaret Griffin. They feed
and water the birds, and enjoy it when the birds visit.

(They also feed and water us, and enjoy it when we visit, too!)

Table of Contents

Introduction

Bird watching may be the most popular and easiest of outdoor activities. It's certainly a favorite of Elizabeth, 8 years old when this was written, and Steve, who turned 41 during that process.

We watched birds on the ocean, along rivers, and in our backyard, while we were writing this book. That gave us extra time together, which we really enjoy.

Wherever you find birds, it's fun to watch them. It's especially fun to feed them and attract them to your yard. Maybe you'll find that one bird is your favorite.

The mourning dove is Elizabeth's favorite kind of bird, and she says she doesn't know why. She just likes them. Steve's favorite bird is the chickadee. He likes it because it seems so cheerful, is willing to come near to people to feed, and stays around all winter in Michigan where the Griffins live. It's easy to watch!

There are hundreds of other kinds of birds, and books that explain lots about each kind. This book talks about YOU watching the birds. It will help you learn their names, and identify them correctly when you see them.

But first—watch the birds. We hope this book makes it easier and more fun. Big and small, pretty and dull, in your yard and far away, birds are special. So are the people who watch them!

Opposite page: Magnolia warbler.

CHAPTER 1
What Is A Bird?

When you see an animal with feathers, that's a bird. Most birds fly, too. There are a few birds, such as kiwis, ostriches, penguins and chickens, that don't fly. But they all have feathers. Kiwis look as if they have fur, but they really have feathers. Even birds with bald heads, like vultures, have feathers on most of their bodies.

Anyway, most birds fly, and all birds have feathers. They all have beaks, too. They all have wings—although penguin wings look like flippers, and that's what they're used for.

All birds hatch from eggs, although the way they make nests is different from one kind of bird to another.

Birds come in all shapes and sizes. That's one of the things that's so interesting about birds—all the different kinds of them.

Birds come in sizes from hummingbirds to albatrosses. The Helena's hummingbird, which lives in Cuba, is just 2-1/4 inches long from the tip of its bill to the tip of its tail, when it's all grown up. It weighs less than one ounce—less than a letter you might get in the mail. Its egg is less than one-half inch long.

The tallest bird alive today is the North African ostrich—some males are 9 feet tall. An ostrich egg can be 8 inches long.

Then there's the albatross. That's the bird with the longest wingspan—the distance from the tip of one wing to the tip of the other wing, stretched right out. An albatross's wings stretch 12 feet. You could take four first-graders and have them stretch their arms out as far as they could. Stand them in line, each one just touching the next person's fingertips. When four kids are lined up, they'll be reaching as far as one albatross with its wings spread!

That's how big a bird can be. What about how heavy? An ostrich can weigh as much as 300 pounds—that's about five second-graders!

Some kinds of birds are plentiful. You probably see lots of sparrows, robins, starlings and mourning doves. Other birds, though, are very rare—whooping cranes, California condors, brown pelicans, Kirtland's warblers. They're endangered. That means

Opposite page: Snow geese.

Brown pelican.

there aren't very many left. They could become extinct—gone completely, forever. That has happened to some birds, like the great auk and the passenger pigeon. Bird watchers were some of the first people to work to protect endangered birds.

Birds come in all different colors. That's one of the main ways we tell different kinds of birds apart. There are drab sparrows, bright cardinals and brilliantly colored rain forest parrots.

Most of a bird's color comes from its feathers. Male birds are often much brighter in color than females of the same species, or kind of bird. That helps the show-off males get the females' attention at breeding time, when more young birds are to be born. The female is often dull, or drab colored. That's so other creatures won't see her so easily and come get the nest and the eggs or the young birds in it.

You've probably found a feather dropped onto the ground by a passing bird. Maybe you've picked it up and studied it. Often, you can guess what kind of bird it came from. Can you guess which part of the bird's body the feather came from? Have you ever looked at a feather with a hand lens? There are some interesting things to learn about feathers.

Feathers are made of keratin, the same material that makes the scales on snakes and lizards, and even the scales on the legs of some birds. Feathers have stems. That's the stiff piece you probably grab first. It runs down the center of the feather.

The stem splits into fine strands, which split into even finer strands. Eventually, all those strands form a feather. Like a fan, it is light but thick enough to catch the wind. That's just what a bird needs. Feathers, all together, form a tight covering for the bird. The feathers and the air they hold inside them keep the cold away from a bird's skin.

That's especially important because birds are warm-blooded creatures like you and me. When they're healthy, their insides are from 105 to 109 degrees F. (41 - 43 degrees C.) That's six to ten degrees warmer than your temperature. Birds live outdoors, and don't have clothes to put on—their feathers have to do a great job of keeping them warm.

There are several kinds of feathers on every bird. Contour feathers help give the bird its shape. Down, between contour feathers and the skin, is a special feathery fluff that keeps birds warm. Flight feathers are the stiff ones on the wings and tail. They press against the wind when the bird is flying to help keep it in the air.

A bird's feathers don't last forever. They wear out, and have to be replaced. The bird just grows new ones, kind of like the way you grow new teeth when your baby teeth come out, or more hair after a haircut.

When birds shed their old feathers and grow new ones, we call it molting. Many birds gradually molt late in the summer. You might notice a feather or two missing on a bird at your feeder, or find a few more shed feathers than usual in your front yard or in the woods. That's nothing compared to what some birds do. Waterfowl—ducks and geese—lose all their flight feathers at once and must hide in thick weeds and other cover. They can't fly away from their enemies until new flight feathers grow.

For those waterfowl, and many other birds, flight feathers and flying are very important. That's how they get to their food, water and resting spots. Some birds fly to different parts of the world as the seasons change. Flying gets them away from danger, too.

Flight feathers are one thing about birds that helps them fly. Another is the special way their bones are formed. Like yours, a bird's skeleton has two legs, two arms (wings), a neck and a skull. There are some differences, though. Your bones have something in them called "marrow," which helps keep you healthy. Birds don't have it

and don't need it. Their bones are hollow, and that makes them a lot lighter. The breast bone of a bird has a ridge or raised line on it. Strong muscles attach to it, to help flap those wings.

Wings can flap really fast, too. The smaller the bird, the faster it beats its wings when it's flying. A hummingbird flaps its wings 50 times every second. That's faster than you can even see. It looks like a blur. Once, we watched a big eagle fly. Its wings beat very slow and even, maybe just once a second. Sometimes large birds can soar, flying like a kite for long periods of time, without even flapping their wings.

Sometimes birds fly for long distances. We call it migration when animals move from one place to another, far away, for a long time. Sometimes a trip can take three months. Birds migrate for many reasons, especially to find the kind of food they need.

Flying, to a bird, requires two different things. Somehow the bird needs to be held up in the air, off the ground. And it needs to move forward. The bird's wings take care of both jobs.

Lift is what we call the way a bird stays up in the air. It does it because of the shape of its wings. If you look closely at a bird's wing, you can see that it is curved on top, kind of like a cup turned upside down. You can see that best near where the wing attaches to the bird's body. (An airplane wing has the same kind of curve, and for the same reason.) When air travels over a shape like this, it moves faster over the top of the curve than underneath it. The little bits of air on top are farther apart, so they do less pushing on the wing. There's more air pressure beneath the wing. That pushes upward on the wing, and the rest of the bird's body is light enough that the push holds it up in the air.

If you look at a mounted bird (maybe in a museum) or a model of one, you might notice that the curve in the wing only comes about half-way out from the body. The outer part, called the wingtip, is much flatter. This part of the wing moves in kind of a semi-circle, a little like a swimmer doing the breaststroke. That pulls the bird forward, just like it does the swimmer, just like an airplane's propeller.

Birds also glide. Broad-winged birds such as eagles and vultures are great at it. The best is the albatross. Its wings are 12 feet across, and it can glide for hours above the sea.

Seeing is almost as important as flying to a bird. That's why birds have such big

15

Opposite page: American woodcock wing close-up.

Barred owl.

eyes. An ostrich's eyes are two inches across! What's to see? Birds want to see the bright colors of other birds. That's one way they communicate, or talk to each other. Peacock feathers, the wing patches on mallards, the red head of a woodpecker—those all help other birds see them.

Different birds have eyes good for different things. Owls fly mostly at night, hunting for meals. They have eyes built especially for seeing when it isn't very light. The world they see is black and white, like early televisions or the photographs inside this book. Other birds, especially birds that are active in the daytime, see colors—but they can't see very well at night.

Some birds see the same thing with both eyes, the way you do. They can judge how far away something is. Many of the birds that have to catch their food see this way. They need to judge distances, the way you need to know how far away a ball is, so you can catch it.

Other birds see different things with each eye. They're the thing other animals want to catch and eat! Don't you wish you could see in different directions when you're trying to hide from your playmates?

Pigeons (or "rock doves") are favorite meals of many other creatures. That's why they can see almost in a full circle. Hawks and owls, which eat things such as pigeons, have eyes that work together to make hunting easier.

Other birds have special eye systems. Woodcocks can see backward and upward, which is handy while they poke the ground with their long beaks, looking for worms. Bitterns can point their beaks straight up in the air and still see—which is great because they hold their heads up perfectly straight in the marsh. They look just like marsh grass, and fool creatures that might be looking for a meal.

Why is the design of the eyes so important? It's because birds can't move their eyes the way you can. Their eyes stay put, and the bird moves its head to see something different. They're very good at it. An owl could sit on your porch looking at one neighbor, turn its head to see the street, keep turning to see the other neighbor, and turn some more to see in the backyard.

You can't turn that far. But then, you're not a bird.

CHAPTER 2
Why Bird Watch?

Most of us pick hobbies that we enjoy and that let us learn new things. Bird watching does both.

And birds are pretty. Well, most of them anyway. Even if they're not exactly what we might call beautiful, their shapes, colors or abilities usually make us say "wow!" Even the turkey vulture, a bird some people call ugly, is impressive as it soars high in the sky in search of a dead creature it might "recycle" into a vulture lunch.

Watching birds fly is fascinating. People wondered, maybe for millions of years, just how birds do that. Now we know how they do it, but we're still impressed.

People have always wanted to fly, and that's one reason they've always enjoyed watching birds. But we can fly only in airplanes or spaceships, or maybe with parasails or other wild equipment. Birds can fly on their own, and that special skill makes it fun to watch them.

Where birds fly is another thing that makes bird watching fun. They fly around our homes—but also, many of them fly thousands of miles away.

Many birds migrate. That means they change their living area by flying to a new spot, a long way away. Some geese spend the summer way up in the Arctic Circle, nibbling green grass and raising their goslings. When winter's coming, though, these geese fly more than a thousand miles south, where waters stay unfrozen and fields aren't covered with snow. When spring returns, they migrate back to the north.

People have tried to figure out what makes a bird migrate—the length of a trip, the bird's size, how well or poorly its feathers insulate it against cold. And none of those seem to make much difference. Birds migrate for food and water. Only those birds that are equipped to find food in the winter—birds with bills designed for seed-cracking, grub digging or fishing—stay "up north" when the snow flies.

So, bird watching also helps us keep track of the season. Where we live, when we hear loudly honking groups of Canada geese, called flocks or flights, we look up. We see them flying overhead in a V-shaped group, and we know that means fall has arrived and we'll be building snowmen soon. Or else, it means the snow will soon be gone and

Opposite page: Black-capped chickadee.

spring's just around the corner.

Groups throughout the continent of North America recently started celebrating International Migratory Bird Day each year, in honor of all the migratory birds—songbirds, shorebirds, raptors and waterfowl.

The U.S. Fish and Wildlife Service says that more than 360 species of birds migrate each year, breeding and raising families in the north and spending the winter in the south.

A special group, called neotropical migrants, travel all the way to Mexico, Central America and the Caribbean to spend the winter. (You might want to get out a map or globe to see how far those trips take them.) About half of North America's migratory birds are neotropicals—including warblers, vireos, orioles, hummingbirds, swallows, swifts, shorebirds and some raptors, or birds of prey.

You might watch other migrants. Eagles, hawks and owls all are well-known for their long migrations. Ducks gather in flocks to fly south. Maybe you've seen ponds just about full of ducks making their way back north in the spring, too!

Some songbirds migrate. In the Great Lakes region, where we live, house finches, bluejays and cardinals visit our feeders all winter. But most robins (who eat lots of worms) fly south when the ground freezes.

Watching the birds and keeping track of which ones are visiting gives one more good way to tell what season it is, without a calendar. Migration gives us a chance to see kinds of birds we don't see at other times of the year.

No matter what season it is, birds are interesting to watch. They do weird things each and every day. You can watch a sparrow chew on a seed—a common bird doing something it does every day. But look closely. It picks up a sunflower seed, cracks it with its beak, takes out the center and eats it. Then, maybe it picks up half of the shell in its mouth, and tries to eat it, and then spits it out. Chances are it will pick up the other half, try to eat that, and spit it out, too. Finally, it will get a brand new seed.

Maybe you'll watch a robin tilt its head trying to hear a worm below the ground, or a finch take a bath in a birdbath or puddle, or an osprey sit atop a tall, strong nest of sticks. Each time you watch birds you'll probably see something new, if you watch closely enough.

Birds, it seems, are always doing something. Coming. Going. Eating. Drinking.

Opposite page: Duck flocks.

Fishing. Arguing. Singing. Sleeping. Bathing in dust or water. Nest-building. Baby raising. Flying. Sitting. Standing.

Certain birds do certain things, and in certain places. That's where the fun of learning comes in. Each bird watching trip will help you know a little more about birds. After awhile you'll know which bird flies a certain way and makes a certain call in a certain area. You'll know the bird before you see it clearly. Then you'll be ready to learn about another one. That's bird watching!

We keep watching and hoping to see something really unusual. One nature writer in a newspaper wrote about watching as a squirrel tried to raid a wren's house to eat those birds' eggs. The wrens made a racket and pecked at the squirrel, and a bluejay and even a robin joined in the fight and drove the squirrel away. That kind of cooperation doesn't happen very often. You want to be watching when it does.

Bird watching can help birds, too. Every year groups of people take part in special "Christmas bird counts" sponsored by the National Audubon Society. They keep track of how many birds of different kinds they see. By comparing the results from year to year, people can tell how things are going for different kinds of birds—and what needs to be done to help birds in need.

These people are often biologists, scientists who study living things. Some biologists spend most of their time working with birds. They're called ornithologists.

Sometimes birds and the wild places where they live need protection. An eagle's nest might be protected by telling people they can't come near it. Beaches where plovers nest might be off-limits to dogs. Finding spots where rare birds live can help protect them and that habitat, or living area.

No matter how young or old, rich or poor, fat or thin, short or tall—one and all, you can bird watch. (You can bird watch even while doing other things; a cardinal peeeer peeered at us while we were writing the sentence before this one.) A bird book and binoculars help, but you don't need anything but your eyes, ears and mind to learn and appreciate birds.

Maybe that's the best reason of all for bird watching. We're here, and the birds are here. We're neighbors on the earth. And getting to know the neighbors is just enjoyable, good manners!

Green-backed heron.

CHAPTER 3
How Do You Bird Watch?

Bird watching is two things, mostly—seeing a bird, and figuring out what kind of bird it is. That's a good way to start, anyway. But sure, there's more to it than that. It's not always easy to see a bird. Maybe it's far away, or small, or maybe it likes to stay away from people.

Sometimes your only clue to a bird might be its sound, or the holes it makes in trees, or its footprints. A feather, or a silhouette (a shape against the sky), or a nest may be all you see.

Then comes figuring out what kind of bird it is. Common birds, the ones you see around your house every day, you'll learn quickly. Chances are, just a few days after you first figure out what kind they are, you'll know instantly what you see.

Yes, the birds we see most often are the ones we identify best. But different birds, like different people, live in different areas. The common birds in your backyard might not be the same ones we see every day.

That's why we're not going to try to teach about lots of certain kinds of birds in this book. We want to talk about people like you, going bird watching for the fun of it.

You might want a special bird guide, with chapters about each kind of bird that lives in your area, to use to identify the birds you see. We've listed some good ones in the back of this book.

Actually, we're not very good at identifying birds ourselves. Often we study a bird, maybe making some notes about it, and check a book later to discover what kind of bird it was, and to learn more about it. You don't have to be great at identifying birds to be a bird watcher—you just have to love watching them!

Remember one thing about bird books, though. They're good because they have clear pictures of each kind of bird. But the birds you see probably won't be that close up, in light that perfect. Sometimes the pictures in bird books were taken in places such as zoos, not backyards. The photographers probably had special cameras that made the birds look really close, using powerful lenses like telescopes. Maybe they're drawings.

So you shouldn't be disappointed if birds don't look really close up to you when

you're outdoors watching them.

Birds also look different at different times of the year. That's especially true about male birds, which are usually the most colorful. Many of them, though, aren't as colorful in the winter as they are in the spring, when it's time to raise another family.

Maybe you've heard of birds called laughing gulls. They're a kind of seagull, and they sometimes fly around with their relatives, the herring gulls. You can tell the laughing gulls from herring gulls by the laughing gulls' black heads—most of the year. We saw them in Maine in the summer, and it was easy to tell what they were. But in the winter they have just a little gray spot on the back of the head. So it's good there are other clues. Laughing gulls laugh. Chuckle, really. And that makes it easy to identify them at any season, even if you can't see them clearly at all!

How else can you identify birds, then, if you can't often see them close up and clearly? There are plenty of good clues.

Field marks are the things about a bird that makes it look different—the way your brother's nose or your sister's hairdo make them look like nobody else but your brother or sister. You won't get to know each bird individually, like you do your brother or sister, but field marks help you learn one kind of bird from another.

Field marks include such features as tail color, shape, pattern or size; leg length, shape or color; bill shape and coloring; color and pattern markings of its feathers and more.

We had fun making a chart of the gulls. The different black and white patterns of each type of gull make a pretty design, and it's easy to see the contrast, what's different about each kind of gull.

Some field marks even give you a pretty good idea of how a bird lives.

Short, round wings make for speedy takeoff and fast flight—for short distances. Long, broad wings are great for soaring high in the sky. Long, slender wings carry a bird in fast flight after flying insects.

Tails are important, and each kind of bird has a certain kind of tail. Studying a tail can help you guess how the bird lives.

A bird's tail helps balance the bird when it's perched, and when it's flying. It serves as a rudder in flight, too, helping the bird change directions the same way a canoe paddle held in the water helps steer a boat.

Different kinds of birds have different kinds of tails. A forked tail, such as the barn swallow's, helps it make graceful flights, with plenty of careful, controlled zigs and zags. That's just what a bird needs for swooping and scooping up insects.

A broad and fanned tail is perfect for soaring. Hawks, eagles, turkey vultures and other high-flying, gliding birds have tails this shape.

Bills are perfectly suited to the life of a bird, too. Slender, pointed bills are great for grabbing bugs. Short and thick bills are sturdy tools for crushing seeds to get at the nutritious meat inside. Long, slender bills poke into the ground to find earthworms for birds such as the woodcock. Short and stout bills are the property of ground feeding birds. Long and sharp bills are spears. Birds such as kingfishers use them to spear fish for their meals.

You'll also learn that feet match a bird's lifestyle. Three webbed toes on each foot help a duck swim. Feet with long, curved "talons" or hook-shaped toes help ospreys grab fish for food. Two toes in front and two in back of each foot help woodpeckers hold on as they climb a tree.

Where a bird lives gives good clues, too. Some birds love cities, others deep, dark

Pileated woodpecker.

forests. Shorebirds are almost always near water. A guidebook usually tells the favorite living areas of each kind of bird.

Many bird books also show silhouettes of birds, the shape you'd get if you traced around one and colored it all in black. Silhouettes of the bird flying and resting make it a lot easier to figure out what kind of bird you've seen.

Sometimes the way a bird acts gives you a hint which one it is. A bird tugging worms from your yard may well be a robin. One soaring over your schoolyard in the evening may just be a nighthawk. Nuthatches scamper up and down tree trunks—upside down! Shorebirds are always bobbing their tails up and down. A killdeer pretends it is injured to protect its young.

Birds have certain flying styles that match the way they live. Basketball players, football players and skaters all move differently. They each move the best way for what they do. It's the same way with birds.

Soaring birds like eagles and vultures are often seen watching for food. They sail like gliders, way up in the sky, ready to dive to earth when they've spotted their next meal. Flycatchers zip this way and that, catching flies. Hummingbirds buzz up, down and sideways from flower to flower. Birds that live in forests fly between thick patches of trees without crashing into any.

Birds make very distinctive sounds—calls that make it clear where their "property" ends and the next bird's begins, and songs that they use at morning and evening, and at certain times of the year. "Bird listening" gets its own chapter, next.

Most of us just like to watch birds, though, and a telescope or binoculars can make that easier. But you really don't need them. You can see plenty of birds, right out of your window.

Telescopes are long tubes with specially-made glass in the front and back and make things look bigger, or closer, than they are. You may hear a serious bird watcher talk about a "spotting scope." That's a telescope especially made to "spot" such far-off things as birds.

Two telescopes fastened together next to each other, one for each of your eyes, is called a set of binoculars. It's amazing, but when the binoculars fit you right, what you see through the two tubes combines into one clear, close-up picture.

Telescopes and binoculars both need to be adjusted to give you a clear picture, "in focus," of what you're looking at. That's usually done by turning a dial or moving a lever. You'll know when you've got it right—the world looks so crisp and clear!

Experts often recommend "7 x 35" binoculars. That means that things you see through them look 7 times larger than if you just looked with your eyes, and that looking through the binoculars you see a pie-shaped chunk of the world of about 35 degrees. If a huge pie was cut into 10 pieces and you were in the center looking through these binoculars, you'd see just about what one of the slices would cover.

Here's a good tip. Look at the bird without the binoculars. Now, lift the binoculars up to your eyes without looking away from the bird. That's the easiest way to get the bird "in view."

For a really good view, you have to adjust the binoculars to you. Like birds, each of us is different, even in the distance between our eyes. To adjust your binoculars, hold them against your face, like you'd look through them. Grab each tube or barrel firmly, and move them closer together or farther apart until you see just one circular picture.

Your eyes are even different—from each other. Many binoculars can be adjusted to match your eyes better.

On most binoculars, you'll see numbers, or plus/minus markings on one of the barrels, at the end you put up to your eye. This is called the diopter setting. Set it to "0," or the middle setting. Now, look at something that's a long way away. Keep both eyes open, but cover the end of the barrel with the setting with one hand. Use the focus wheel or lever between the barrels to make the picture clear.

Now, cover the other lens, and use the diopter setting—not the focus wheel or lever—to make the picture clear again. Look at the setting you've discovered is right for your eyes, and remember it. Maybe even write it down. The next time you use the binoculars, you won't have to do all this over again.

Even if nobody borrows your binoculars and resets them, the diopter setting gets bumped out of adjustment easily.

Binoculars cost a lot of money, and are worth taking good care of. Store them with the eyecups up, and make sure they don't get dropped or banged around. Keep them where it's cool and dry. To clean binoculars, use an air puffer or special "canned air" from a camera shop to blow away dust or dirt, or use a soft lens brush. To remove dirt or fingerprints, use a soft cotton cloth, rubbing gently in a circular motion.

If you're not sure, ask a camera shop or sports shop clerk how to clean or adjust your binoculars or telescope. Never try to take one apart. You might ruin it.

Almost every town has a bird watching or nature club. Some schools teach special night classes in bird watching. Or you can check at places such as elevators or shops selling bird seed for tips on what birds live in your area, and the best ways to get a look at them. Bird sanctuaries and wildlife refuges are great places to learn and practice bird watching.

You can watch birds in your backyard, or you can watch them from a boat on the ocean. Canoeing is a great way to see birds. So is going to a nature center. Or tending a bird feeder at school. Birds are everywhere. We just have to watch for them.

It's important to know what NOT to do when bird watching, too. Someday, you'll probably find a baby bird that looks as if it's been abandoned. You'll want to pick it up and take care of it. DON'T!

It's against the law to keep almost any bird taken from the wild, unless you get special training and a permit from your state Department of Natural Resources or the U.S. Fish and Wildlife Service. Wildlife recovery groups, which do have these permits and training, might be able to help. Check in the telephone book under "wildlife."

Chances are good that the parent bird is nearby. He or she will probably look after the youngster as soon as you leave. If it's truly all alone, you probably can't save it.

You might find a baby bird without feathers, and know where the nest is. You could put that bird back in the nest, and then leave it alone. Chances are, the parent will come back and take care of it. That's the best way to take care of a little bird—to let Mother Nature do it.

Opposite page: Double-crested cormorant.

CHAPTER 4
Bird Listening

It sounds funny, but one of the most important things about bird watching isn't watching at all. It's listening.

Most birds make sounds. If you listen for and learn those sounds, you can learn a lot about the birds and what they are doing.

Most birds make two different kinds of sounds—calls and songs. Some make other sounds, too, such as the air-drumming of a ruffed grouse, or the rat-a-tat of a woodpecker on a pole. We'll talk a little more about them later.

Experts say that no animals except people have more complicated sound signals than birds. They use sounds to tell rival or unfriendly birds to stay away. Sounds are used to tell their mates and young birds where to find them, and to convince other birds that might become their mates that they're very special birds.

Most birds have calls—short buzzes, chirps, cheeps or other sounds that are simple. Almost every young bird makes calls that tell its parents it's healthy, and begging for some chow. If you have a little brother or sister—really little—you know they know how to beg for food, loudly. Just like little humans, little birds seem to know those songs without having to learn them. We call that instinct. Other calls are learned.

Experts say that on some islands in the ocean, where as many as one million seabirds might live close together in a rookery, a parent bird can pick out its own chick just by the sound of its begging call. If that's not surprising enough, a chick—even before it hatches from the egg—learns to tell the sound of its parent's call from those of any other bird.

Different birds make different calls, for different reasons. A female ptarmigan, which lives in Arctic regions, makes a call that instantly sends its youngsters scattering and looking for cover. A female bobwhite quail has a call that does the opposite. Her chicks gather close to her for protection from danger.

A pair of adult birds might use what are called social calls. These are sounds they make just to keep track of each other while they wander around looking for food. They stay together, but not so close that they're in each other's way.

Opposite page: Western meadowlark.

Birds that migrate often fly long distances at night. They use special calls to keep track of each other while flying along. Again, the idea is to stay together, but not too close.

Sometimes the sound of a call gives us a pretty good idea what it means. Scientists tell us that calls made to scare off intruders or settle a fight are lower, buzzier or growlier than those used for other messages.

Different calls for different purposes: a chickadee perched in a tree calls "chickadee" at a cat on the ground. You'll probably hear a high-pitched "sseeee" if there's a hawk in the sky. The higher-pitched sound is harder for the hawk to trace to the bird. A chickadee in a tree isn't in much danger from a cat on the ground—but it is in danger from a hawk in the air.

Many songbirds have a lot of calls. Some have 15 different ones!

Calls are handy. They're short, and don't require much energy. That's important for a bird because they're small and constantly burn up energy. Bird song is a lot more complicated. Their melodies are pretty, and it takes a lot of energy to make them. It's like the difference between you shouting "Hey, you!" at someone messing with your bike and singing your mother a complicated love song.

People who study bird songs keep track of how many different ones a species, or kind of bird, sings. The brown thrasher has more than 1,000 different songs, these scientists have found. Birds seem to know many of their songs by instinct. They have to learn other songs from other birds of the same species.

All that singing does two things. A song is meant to attract a mate, guard a bird's territory, or both. Males do most of the singing in the bird world.

Birds do most of their singing at daybreak and sunset. People have often chuckled when, during an eclipse (when the moon or earth blocks the sun and it gets dark outside at an unusual time) birds sing more. But then, the same thing makes people turn on their headlights and do twilight things, too!

There are several ways to learn which birds make which sounds. You can buy or borrow tapes or other recordings of bird songs and calls, and listen to the sound of each kind of bird. You can carefully watch birds in your yard or at a nature center and listen closely for the sounds they make. You might even try taping your neighborhood birds yourself.

A good way to remember what birds sound like is to make up words that sound like

Black-capped chickadee.

the calls and songs.

Cardinals make a sound like "birdy-birdy-birdy." When you hear those words, start looking for a bright red bird.

The robin makes a sound like "cherlee, cherloo."

The bobwhite sounds like "bob white."

The chickadee sounds like "chickadee-dee-dee"—most of the time. Like many birds, it has more than one sound. It also makes a sad, soft "Ooh-hoo."

Many bird books list the words that their authors say sound like the birds. Maybe you'll try them and agree. Maybe you'll come up with one that—to you, at least—sounds closer.

Some birds have different ways of sending messages to each other. Woodpeckers don't use songs to claim their territory or attract mates. They have a drumbeat they make with their bills, thumping on hollow trees or posts. (Sometimes they hammer on metal posts, or even the siding of houses. That drives people crazy!)

A male ruffed grouse, living in the forest, hops up on a fallen log and cups his wings. He then flaps them fast, making little popping noises in the air that sound like hollow drumming. Other male grouse know he's ready to protect his area. Female grouse know he's looking for a mate.

Birds make all kinds of noises. Turkeys gobble. Crows caw. Seagulls scream. Warblers sing. Learning which bird makes which sound, and why, is part of the fun of bird watching—even if we can't see the bird we're "watching."

Ruffed grouse drumming on a log.

CHAPTER 5
The Nest

Birds don't leave many signs of where they've been. The one you're most likely to see while bird watching is a nest.

Nests are shelters in which birds lay their eggs and raise their young. Birds make them in almost every shape, and from just about every kind of material, that you could imagine.

Birds build nests perfect for them and their environment. Small birds like hummingbirds build nests as small as marshmallows. Big birds like eagles build ones as big as a sandbox. They all build nests from the materials they find nearby.

There are open nests on the ground, nests in holes in trees, and hanging nests. A tree in your yard may have a nest in the crook of a branch. Maybe there's one hanging where the roof of your house or apartment building hangs over the wall.

Sparrows always build nests between the panels of the sign in front of a little store in our neighborhood. They're protected there, and the lights help keep them warm.

What are nests made of? Twigs, mud, string, spider webs or combinations of these materials are common. A friend of ours who worked building highways even found a nest some hard-working bird had woven from left-over pieces of tough wire! We can't imagine how it did it, and we never learned what kind of bird it was.

People sometimes notice that they see a lot of birds, but not a lot of bird nests. Nests are usually hidden really well in brush, and trees, and tall grass. That's good, when you think about it.

Bird nests are often camouflaged, or made to look like their surroundings. Maybe you've seen a bird flying with a long piece of grass in its beak. That's likely to become a piece of its nest. Birds often make their nests out of things they find, the same kind of things that are over the area where the nest is built. That makes it hard for other animals to see the nest. Since many other animals eat bird eggs or young birds, that's a very good thing.

Sometimes both parents build the nest. Sometimes just one or the other. Birds do all their nest building with just their beaks and legs. (Can you image building or decorat-

Opposite page: Eastern bluebird.

ing your bedroom, or even just cleaning it, using only your mouth and your feet?)

You can often see birds carrying materials to their nests. If you put out some materials, the birds might use them. Short pieces of yarn or string, or clumps of lint from the clothes dryer, will often be grabbed by nesting birds if you hang them in trees and bushes in the spring. We've often seen nests with garbage bag ties, pieces of bread-wrapper, or discarded ribbons woven into them.

The bigger the bird, the sturdier the nest. Eagles and ospreys use big sticks to make large nests—and they (or other birds of the same kind) use them year after year.

Other birds, such as mourning doves, build nests that are quite flimsy, and usually used just once. Mourning dove nests are so flimsy that sometimes storms blow them down, and the doves have to rebuild them during the season. If eggs or young birds are lost when a nest collapses, the doves lay and raise more.

Among migratory birds, the male often arrives first to claim a territory. It sings loud and long, telling every other bird he's the boss, and hoping his showing off brings the attention of a female. This happens in spring—a great time to learn the sounds of all kinds of birds.

One kind of seabird, the guillemot, nests on rocky shelves and islands. Its eggs are pear-shaped, so that if they start to roll they don't roll far. That's good, because guille-mots usually lay just one egg.

Nests can be shallow depressions scratched in the ground. Mallards, like many other birds, line this kind of nest with a little bit of grass or leaves. Eider ducks use their own down feathers to pad their nests.

Ruffed grouse, birds of the forest, simply lay their eggs in a little cluster of leaves and grass on the forest floor. Other gamebirds, such as pheasants, woodcocks and wild turkeys, do the same thing.

A killdeer lays her eggs on the ground. If you get too close, she'll run off, pretend-ing she has a broken wing. Chances are, you or another "predator" will follow her and not notice the eggs or young. She also squawks like crazy, to get your attention away from her nest.

Birds in other parts of the world have some unusual nest-building tricks.

Some birds build very strong nests from cement-like mixes of earth or sand and other things. In South America, the ovenbird makes a cement of sand and cow manure

Frosted nest.

to make its hollow nest.

The tailorbird uses its beak to sew leaves together into a pouch nest. Weaverbirds loop, tie and thread strips of such things as grass or leaves into a nest. Sometimes many weaverbirds pitch in to weave one big nest for many birds. They have little individual chambers inside, kind of like apartments for the birds that live there.

Most birds sit on nests to hatch eggs, but some build incubators! Megapodes, which means "large-footed" birds, live in Australia and New Guinea. They cover their eggs with piles of leaves and stuff. As this material rots, it produces heat, just like a backyard compost pile does. That heat helps hatch the eggs!

Emperor penguins—mom and dad—balance the egg under a fold of skin on their feet.

Most of the birds that live in the United States and the rest of North America use nests of some sort, and many of them are the woven-stick kind we usually think of. There are many different kinds, though.

Robins cement their nests with mud. An oriole nest hangs from a tree limb and looks like a round purse or small beach bag.

45

Opposite page: Cliff swallow.
Above: Osprey.

If you want to see bird nests, the best time to look is in winter. Then the leaves are off the trees. Remember, birds only use nests for raising young. They don't live in them, the way we live in houses. They don't sleep in them once the young birds are gone.

In winter, the adults and the young birds, now grown up, are gone. You can study what looks like the magic of nest-making.

One reason for a nest is warmth. Eggs must be kept warm to hatch. Baby birds need to stay warm, too.

One day we were watching a baby sparrow poking its head out of a nesting box we had made and set up several years earlier. It was peeping—peep, peep—and it was bald! Some baby birds have feathers on them right from the start. Some grow them later. Little birds, without good feather coverings, need a nest to keep them warm.

The smaller the bird, the more it needs a nest, too. Small animals have a harder time keeping warm. (It's like when you break a big cookie into smaller pieces. It cools quicker than if left in one big chunk. But cool cookies are great; cold birds aren't.)

So hummingbirds must build especially well insulated nests to keep their teeny-tiny chicks warm. They use spider webs, plant hairs and wool to build a nest about as big as a quarter.

We once saw an osprey's nest. It had been used for more than 50 years by different ospreys, and was as tall as a garage, wider than a sandbox.

Bird nests, small and big, have plenty in common: they're shelters birds build to safely raise their young.

Opposite page: Blue Jay and young.

CHAPTER 6
Where to Bird Watch
Part 1: Getting the Birds to Come to You

One good way to watch birds is to invite them to come to you. There are several things that birds need, that you can offer them—food, shelter, water and a place to hatch their young.

Birds find much of their food naturally—seeds from trees and other plants, grubs and other insects in all the places they hide, and berries wherever they grow. They'll gladly come to food you provide them, too. That makes it easy to watch them, while you're helping them.

Your foods are especially helpful to birds in the winter and spring. In winter, many of the foods that birds would normally find are covered by ice or snow. That's why many birds fly south for the winter. Some of them will stay around longer, though, if there's food available at places like a bird feeder in your yard.

If you start feeding birds in the winter, you should continue right through the spring. They depend on you. In the summer, they'll keep coming to your feeder, but not as often. They're finding their own food, with bugs and other things available.

More birds will come to your feeder in the spring. They're coming back from their winter spots. They're going to build nests and lay eggs, and they need a lot of food to do that. There's not much food available in the spring, either. The bugs and seeds and stuff like that isn't ready yet, and the birds need to get fat and need lots of energy to do their work!

Different kinds of birds need different foods. Variety in food will bring you more kinds of birds.

Chickadees, nuthatches, flickers, wrens, woodpeckers and many other birds love suet, a hard fat, especially if it's mixed with seeds or cornmeal. Goldfinches flock around thistle seed; their beaks are the perfect shape to snatch that tiny seed from a feeder. Black, oily sunflower seeds are the favorites of many birds. Cracked corn or other seed

49

scattered on the ground will draw ground-feeding birds, such as mourning doves, quail, woodpeckers and juncos.

Birds love bagels—even stale ones. Tie a string through the middle, and hang it up. Watch to see which birds eat it.

Pine cones make good feeders. You can tie a string around the top to hang it. Smear peanut butter into the cracks. Dip it in corn meal, then seed—or just seed—and hang it up. The birds love it.

Pine cones also make good ways to offer nest-building stuff. Stick on short strings or lint. Pieces of fabric or ribbon work, too. The birds will come and pick up the pieces and make nests out of them.

Certain birds rely on certain kinds of foods. Hummingbirds, which drink nectar from brightly colored flowers, will come to a special feeder that offers them fresh nectar, sugar water you can mix or purchase. Orioles will nibble at pieces of orange or other fruit in your yard.

Some people plant bushes that will grow berries birds love—crab-apples, mulberries and others are great natural bird feeders.

There are two good reasons to

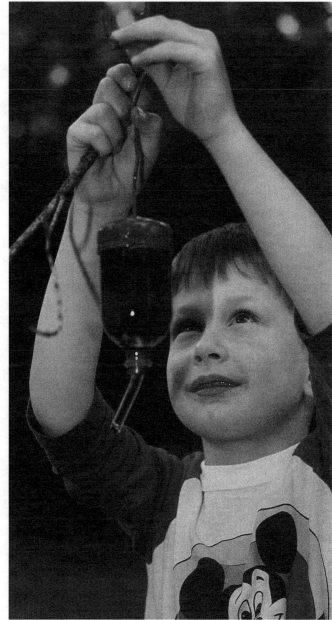

feed birds. One, you can help the birds. Two, you can see them clearly. We like feeders in the yard. We really like a board just outside the kitchen window, though, that has a suet feeder and a little sunflower seed feeder on it. Chickadees, sparrows and finches land just outside the glass, enjoying a snack while we get a real close-up look at them. We plan to add a peanut butter feeder soon.

You can buy feeders from bird watching stores and many other stores, and they work great. You can also build your own feeder. A plastic milk jug, with a hole the size of a softball cut in one side, works great. Hang it from a tree, and stash some seed in it, and the birds will fly in and eat. It's funny to see the milk jug wiggling around when there's a bird in it, eating.

There are other ways to recycle while bird feeding. You can buy metal fittings that screw onto a plastic pop bottle, where the cap used to be. These have feeding holes and posts that make it a perfect feeder. A wire that comes with it makes it easy to hang the feeder.

An onion or potato bag works great to hold suet, which you can buy at a meat counter or meat market.

Sometimes we feed birds without meaning to. Every day, flocks of birds raid

Male Downy woodpecker
on suet feeder.

the food bowl of our dog, who just sits in his kennel in the backyard and watches.

Sometimes people who feed birds find that birds crash into their windows. If you have this problem, try taping a hawk-shaped piece of black paper or plastic on the window. That will scare birds away from your window. Streamers that flap in the wind, or a shiny piece of tin foil, might help, too.

At your feeders, don't put out more feed than birds can use right away. Especially in the hot summer, food that is out there too long can spoil or become contaminated with germs. You could harm or even kill the birds you want to help. Most bird foods stay good for several days.

Hummingbird nectar, which is mostly sugar mixed in water, maybe with red or orange food coloring to attract birds, needs to be changed especially often. It spoils rapidly. The feeder needs to be carefully washed, too.

Besides food, birds need water. Set up a bird bath in your yard, and keep the bath clean and the water fresh, and you'll laugh as you watch the birds splash and drink by sipping water and holding their heads up high.

Some people even build water fountains for birds, or make tinklers that drip water. Birds seem to love the sound of tinkling water. Every time we wash the car, water the garden, or fill the wading pool, the birds start singing like crazy. You'll see more birds by offering water, even if you don't feed them.

Don't forget water in the winter if you live where its gets snowy and icy. The birds might have a tough time finding water that's not frozen, unless you put it out for them.

Birds like to dust themselves in sand, too. Spreading sand on their feathers gets rid of bugs and dirt. Placing a container of dusty sand might increase the number of birds that visit—or the funny things you see them do!

Shelter is another thing birds need. You can provide natural shelter by planting shrubs or leaving brush in place. Some people who have live Christmas trees in their homes place them in the yard after the holidays, to provide a little more cover for the birds.

You can make shelters for birds. We used to talk about bird houses, but that can give people the wrong idea. Birds don't really live in houses. They'll use them as nesting boxes for raising their young.

Nesting boxes can help birds, and can draw them to your neighborhood. Head for the library for books on making boxes for the birds you want. Every kind of bird has its own "dream house," and the wrong box won't attract the birds you want.

Some house-building projects have really helped birds. Eastern bluebirds are much more common now, thanks to thousands of boxes placed on posts about four feet off the ground. Wood ducks once nested in hollow trees. But hollow trees got scarce, and they've learned to raise young wood ducks in wooden or plastic boxes set up for them by people.

It is possible to have too many bird houses in a small area, though, especially if they're for the same kind of bird. Many birds are territorial, meaning they like to have space between them and their neighbors.

Pack birds too tightly by placing too many nesting boxes, and they'll be squabbling, making too much noise for you and using up too much of their valuable energy. The biggest problem is between birds of the same kind. Wrens especially like their own "space." Many bird books list the size of a species' breeding territory. Use that as a guide when setting up nesting boxes for that species.

Some birds will come to a call. You can buy a little call that you twist to make chirps of every kind. Or you can try kissing the back of your hand to make a "birdy" sound, and see which birds come to see what all the noise is about!

You'll see your visitors best if they don't see you first. Indoors, don't make a lot of quick movements near the window. Don't expect as many visitors if there's a big old cat in the window watching, either—although birds will eventually learn that Kitty can't catch them.

Outdoors, try using a blind, a structure behind which you hide.

You can stick a straight umbrella handle into the ground or hold it in a bucket. Then pin fabric around the sides and let it drape down. Cut or leave holes to look through. The birds can't see you—and rain can't get you. And, best of all, you can see the birds. Your neighbors may laugh, but the birds won't. They don't know you're there, remember?

A play tent makes a good blind in the yard, too. You can even read, if you want, while waiting for the birds. You'll hear them peeping or chomping on food. Maybe you'll want to read about birds, until the birds arrive.

RETZER NATURE CENTER TRAIL HEAD

TRAIL ORIENTATION MAP

LEGEND•

- ADVENTURE TRAIL (.20 MI)
- PRAIRIE POND TRAIL (.40 MI)
- PRAIRIE VISTA TRAIL (.70 MI)
- SELF-GUIDING NATURE TRAIL (.45 MI)
- GENERAL HIKING TRAIL (.90 MI)
- BROWN'S FEN TRAIL (1.50 MI)
- ORCHARD TRAIL (.75 MI)
- X-C SKI TRAIL (WINTER ONLY, 1.10 MI)

• MILEAGE GIVEN IS ROUND-TRIP
  DISTANCE FROM TRAILHEAD

YOU ARE HERE

ADVENTURE TRAIL

HOW TO USE THE ADVENTURE TRAIL

TRAIL BROCHURES AND INFORMATION

CHAPTER 7
Where to Bird Watch
Part 2: Going to the Birds

Many kinds of birds can be convinced to come see us. Feeders, nesting boxes, water and shelter near our homes will attract birds. We enjoy watching them go about their daily activities.

We can go to where the birds are, too. Then we get to see new places, as well as new birds.

Sometimes birds are in places where it's easy to go see them. Sometimes not.

One of our favorite bird watching places is a nature center. It has a bird feeding area with a big wall of windows. Outside are several kinds of feeders with many kinds of seeds. A special coating on the glass lets us see the birds, but they can't see us.

At this nature center's viewing area, a microphone outside catches the sounds of the birds and plays them on a speaker so we can learn their calls and songs. There are comfortable chairs, and a bird guide book so we can figure out which ones are which. There's even a blackboard where people write down the names of the birds they see. It's fun to watch for one that hasn't been put on the list yet for the month!

If we have questions, we can write them down, post them on a board, and come back a few days later to learn the answer. There are people called naturalists who work there. Their job is to explain nature things to people.

That kind of bird watching is comfortable and fun any time of the year, any time of the day. Sometimes bird watching is a little tougher.

During the summer in which we wrote this book, we took a boat trip to an island in the Atlantic ocean. We wanted to see seabirds—puffins, cormorants, eiders, terns, guillemots. We did see most of them, on a boat built especially to take large groups of people near these Maine islands.

A boat trip like that is a great way to learn more about birds. Our guide, a naturalist, told us that one of the islands was named Egg Rock, because people who lived on the island hundreds of years ago collected seabird eggs to eat, instead of chicken eggs.

King eider.

That's one of the reasons the birds need protection now.

There are other reasons, too—people killed birds for their feathers, to decorate hats, and chemical pollution hurt them, too.

Some of these islands, like other places around the country, are now bird sanctuaries, places kept safe just for the birds.

Our guide told us many interesting things, and we got to see some of the birds, but the air was very foggy, and the sea very rough. A lot of the time we don't see birds as close as we want to, or as close as they look in a picture. We did get a pretty good idea how hardy these birds have to be to live in such a harsh environment, or area.

It reminded us again that we don't always get to see birds in real life as colorfully and clearly as we see them in books, in videos or television shows. Seeing their pictures and seeing them again in their natural homes is best of all!

If you want to watch birds where they live, the first step is to learn as much as you can about certain birds. Study the range maps in guide books. They show where in the world each kind of bird can be found in summer and winter.

Then read to see what kind of place within that range the bird likes best. Seashore? Marshes? Deep, tall forests? Open fields? To spot the bird of your choice, you'll

Female cardinal.

61

need to do some homework. It's really fun when you finally see just the bird you're after.

Or, you can do it a different way. Visit an area, spot its birds, and notice their field marks. Then use the guide book and its range maps and habitat descriptions to figure out what birds you've seen.

Canoeing is a great way to bird watch. On one three-hour canoe trip we saw these birds: great blue heron, belted kingfisher, barn swallow, northern or Baltimore oriole, swans, spotted sandpipers, plovers, kingbirds, flycatchers, cardinal, thrush, grackles and robins. It was fun to write down all the birds we saw when we finished the trip.

Later that day, we saw wrens and heard flickers and pileated woodpeckers, and even watched a bald eagle soar overhead as we fished! We added them to our list.

But don't get the idea we're great at identifying birds. We each watched for as many field marks as we could see, then got out a bird book later to help figure out what they all were. One bird darted through the sky, catching insects. We noticed a band of white on its tail. Our guide book told us it was a kingbird. What a fun way to learn about birds!

Someday, maybe we'll know them without looking them up. But even now, it's like figuring out a mystery or solving a puzzle—lots of fun!

Migratory birds offer a special challenge for those who want to go to where the birds are.

Migration is when animals move from one place to another, far away, for a long time. Sometimes the trip can take three months! Birds migrate to eat, have babies, and live in the kind of weather they're suited for. Otherwise they'd just stay in one good spot.

Scientists watch migratory birds very closely. They need special habitat in several areas over the entire year, and a problem in just one spot can mean big trouble. Maybe there's no food for them, or perhaps there's a pollution problem. The biologists who watch migratory birds are learning better ways to keep track of birds and detect pollution problems all the time.

They recently learned how to study the chemicals in the tail feathers of some birds. They think they'll be able to tell where a bird was born (New England, Great Lakes, or the Southeast United States, for example) by the chemicals in its feathers.

If birds from one area aren't as healthy, or there aren't as many of them as there

Opposite page: Great egret.

should be, scientists can start solving the problem.

To watch migratory birds you need to learn which birds pass through your area, and where they stop to rest. Wildlife and waterfowl refuges often provide food and resting cover to migratory birds. Check with a state conservation officer or a U.S. Fish and Wildlife Service official for tips on where to watch migratory birds.

The best places are well-known, attracting birds and bird watchers every year. A local nature club, bird watching group or nature center probably puts together visits to the best spots near you every year.

Whatever kind of bird you're going to go watch, remember that other natural critters live there, too. Mosquitoes and other biting bugs, for example.

Be sure to pack and use mosquito and black fly repellent. The strongest one has a chemical called DEET. For young people's skin, most experts now suggest using something milder, such as citronella, and to use the DEET only on clothing. (Make sure the DEET won't hurt the clothing, first.) Long-sleeved shirts and long pants, rugged shoes and a good hat will protect you from briars. Learn to identify poison ivy and stay away from it. Use proper clothing and sunscreen to keep from getting burned.

Don't get lost! If you're headed into the wild, make sure you know where you're going, and that a big person knows, too. Learn to use a map and compass, and don't get so excited about the birds you've found that you get lost.

Sometimes, we can't go to where the birds are. Sometimes, they need to be protected. The tiny Kirtland's warbler nests in our state. Only about 1,000 of these birds are alive in the whole world, and they all raise their young in the jack pine forests of northern Michigan. Unless you're on a special tour, you can't go into the areas where these little birds nest. There are signs all around telling you to keep out.

Elsewhere, people aren't allowed near piping plover or eagle nesting areas, or the places where other endangered birds are found. Even if a bird species isn't threatened or endangered, we want to always make sure that by going to its home to watch, we're not interfering with the bird's life.

It's tough, but sometimes showing respect for nature's creatures means leaving them alone.

*Opposite page: **Bosque del Apache National Wildlife Refuge.***

CHAPTER 8
Types of Birds: Songbirds

Songbirds are among the favorite birds of many bird-watchers. Most of them are small, many migrate, and their calls and songs make us smile.

The songbirds are also called passerines, or perching birds. Did you ever wonder how a bird that perches, or rests on a tree limb, sleeps without falling off? Well, the weight of the bird makes the bird's ankle joint bend, and that clamps its toes tightly around the limb or perch. The bird has to wake up and lift itself a little to release the "lock" on the perch.

Naturalists are pretty picky about the birds they call "songbirds." They include birds such as thrushes, orioles, tanagers, grosbeaks, catbirds, vireos, buntings and the many kinds of warblers.

Some other great singers—birds we might often call songbirds although they're not officially songbirds—are flycatchers, cuckoos, whippoorwills, hummingbirds and, most common of all, robins.

Many of the songbirds—200 species of them, in fact—migrate from summer habitat to winter habitat. Many are what biologists call neotropical migrants, birds that spend their winters far to the south, near the tropics.

Some of these birds are having troubles. Biologists say the numbers of many kinds of songbirds have fallen. Chemical pollution that harms the birds may be one reason. Another may be the cutting down of Latin American rain forests, where these birds spend their winters. In North America, including the United States, more and larger cities mean fewer forested areas these birds need.

Songbirds have other problems.

Other birds, such as crows, grackles and bluejays eat the eggs and young of some songbirds. Raccoons eat some, too. Cats that are allowed to roam outdoors like to hunt and eat songbirds; that's why cat owners who also love birds put bells on the collar of their cat to warn the birds there's danger nearby.

Birds such as brown-headed cowbirds make it rough on songbirds in a different way. The cowbird lays its big egg in the nest of another bird. Its egg, tended by the other

Opposite page clockwise from top left:
Indigo bunting, Warbling virio,
Robin, Wood thrush.

Kirtland's warbler.

bird, hatches first. The fast-growing young cowbird may push the other eggs or young out of the nest, or eat all the food. Often, the songbird's young don't survive.

For all those reasons, numbers of many of the neotropical songbirds has fallen. The number of wood thrushes, for example, fell about one-fourth between 1980 and 1994. That means that where there were 100 thrushes in 1980, there would be just 75 now.

Maybe bird watchers don't see the difference. Plenty of beautiful, sweetly-singing birds still come to the feeder. But maybe, since you now know songbirds need help, you'll decide to put out a nesting box next spring.

Some songbirds don't use nesting boxes. People have found other ways to help them.

There are many warblers. Some of them are common. Some of them are rare. In Michigan we have the Kirtland's warbler, an endangered species that nests only in the northern part of our state, in scrubby looking jack pine trees. It migrates south each winter to spend the cold months in the lovely Bahamas.

Kirtland's warblers nest on the ground, so they need places where rainwater drains away. They only build nests beneath dense stands of the jack pines, trees that are just 12 to 20 years old, much younger than many forests.

The best way for new forests of jack pines to grow is for old ones to be burned. The heat from the fire opens up the pine cones, releasing seeds to grow into more trees. In northern Michigan, biologists once built fires on purpose to help the warblers. Some fires got out of control, though. Now, thousands of young trees started in nurseries are planted so they'll grow into just the right kind of nesting cover for these warblers.

People help the warblers in another way. They have to stay out of the warbler's nesting areas during the nesting season, unless they have special permission.

In 1994, biologists found more Kirtland's warblers in Michigan than ever before. They traveled warbler country and counted the number of males they heard "singing" courtship songs—601 of them! They figure there's a female warbler for each male, for a total of 1,202. That was the highest since 1961, and a lot better than the 167 counted in 1974 and again in 1987.

In a nesting box, at a bird feeder, or on the jack pine forest floor, people really like keeping track of songbirds.

Evening grosbeak.

CHAPTER 9
Types of Birds: Water Birds

All birds need water. Some birds, though, need lots of water—rivers, streams, lakes or oceans. We call these water birds. They include waterfowl or ducks and geese, plus gulls, shorebirds, seabirds, loons, cranes and more.

Ducks and geese are really suited to life on and around the water. They spread oil on their feathers to make them waterproof. Adult waterfowl get that oil from a gland on their body. Putting it on is called preening. The mother duck puts it on her ducklings. When a duck or goose's feathers are properly oiled, the bird doesn't get wet, even swimming in the water!

Almost everyone knows what the Canada goose looks like. Its black, gray and white markings show up very clearly. Even if you can't see the markings of an individual goose, when a big V-shaped flock of honking geese flies overhead late at night, it's a pretty good sign that spring or fall is here!

Waterfowl also include swans, some of our most beautiful birds. Like other birds, they've been troubled by pollution and other problems, but they're doing better now, too. People are seeing endangered trumpeter swans in places where they haven't been seen in more than 100 years.

One trumpeter swan spotted near Detroit came to Michigan as an egg from Alaska. It was raised in a sanctuary, or safe place, for two years, then released. A little later, it was seen almost 200 miles away. Some of the water birds are good travelers!

Known as the largest species of waterfowl in the world, the trumpeter swan was down to as few as 66 in the entire United States. Biologists say there are now about 1,000 trumpeter swans in the Lower 48 states of the U.S., about 1,000 more in western Canada, and about 12,000 in Alaska.

Field marks help us tell related groups of birds apart. That really helps with the swans. We can compare kinds of swans, and tell which is which by the way they're different. Endangered trumpeter swans are bigger, with big, flat, black bills. They hold their necks straight. Mute swans aren't endangered. They're plentiful. You'll know them when you see them because they each have a large black knob above an orange bill, and

Opposite page: Common eider.

71

Trumpeter swan.

an S-shaped neck.

Some water birds do things that are really unusual. Eiders are a kind of duck. Unlike other birds that leave the nest to eat once in a while, the mother eider duck sits for 30 days without leaving. When the young eiders hatch, the mother is too tired to take care of them. So female eiders without duck-lings of their own take care of groups of youngsters, while the mothers rest, eat and grow strong again. One of these groups of eider babies is called a creche, or kindergarten.

Cormorants are big, black water birds, with long beaks just right for grabbing fish. They dive underwater and can stay there for a minute if they want while they search for fish. And do they like fish!

Biologists say one cormorant eats about one pound of fish every day! Like many birds that live near water, cormorants had rough times in the 1950s and 1960s, when chemical pol-lutants poisoned them. Now they're returning. That's good news, even if people who fish complain that the cor-morants are catching too many!

Loons are fish-eaters, too. These beautiful birds are twice as big as cor-morants, and they eat twice as much—

up to two pounds of fish per day. Loons especially like quiet, clean waters with plenty of fish. Their call, sad and eerie to us, is a sound of the wilderness.

Puffins are wild-looking water birds. One kind that lives in Alaska looks as if it has a wild, spiked-up hairdo!

Cranes, swans, ducks, geese and other big water birds get a lot of attention, but for fun you can't beat watching shorebirds such as common sandpipers. These birds dash on skinny legs, scampering in the waves with bobbing tails in search of food, and scooting out of the way before the next wave comes along.

It's fun spending part of a day just watching to see if the sandpiper dodges the waves successfully every time.

Tufted puffin.

73

CHAPTER 10
Types of Birds: Raptors

Birds that pursue birds and other animals for their food are called birds of prey, or raptors. They include eagles, hawks and owls. They're some of our best-known birds.

So much of the bird news a few years ago was sad. There were fewer and fewer birds flying wild, especially birds of prey. Lately, there's been good news.

The bald eagle, the national symbol of the United States, was recently taken off the official "endangered" species list and put on the "threatened" list instead. That's great. That means extinction, or the loss of every last eagle, doesn't appear as likely as it once did.

People are taking better care of the waters and fish on which eagles depend, as well as keeping areas safe and quiet for the big, beautiful birds.

People once grew up and watched their children grow up, without seeing a single eagle. Now you can almost surely see one this year, if you keep your eyes open.

The bald eagle is the largest member of the North American hawk family. The U.S. Congress named it the national bird in 1782. The bald eagle is 34 to 43 inches long, and its wings stretch as much as 7 1/2 feet from tip to tip.

Almost everything the eagle eats is fish, but it sometimes eats waterfowl, small mammals, or other creatures that have been killed by something else.

You're most likely to see an eagle while it's flying. A mature bald eagle has a white head. All adult bald eagles have a white tail.

Another stunning raptor is the peregrine falcon. This hunting bird roams the skies, spotting prey, or smaller animals, it can catch and eat. It drops upon that prey at speeds of up to 200 miles per hour. Sometimes peregrines knock their prey to the ground—sometimes they kill it in midair.

Peregrine falcons are endangered. At one point around 1960, there were no young peregrines being born in the eastern United States.

People hurt the falcons in several ways. Some people stole young falcons from their nests. Others trapped or shot them. People once thought that birds of prey should be killed, because they killed other creatures. Most people now know that eagles, hawks,

Opposite page: Bald eagle.

owls and falcons are part of a balanced world, part of wildlife diversity.

Chemical pollution also caused problems for the peregrines, just as it did for other raptor species. Chemicals get concentrated in the food chain, where plants and smaller creatures are eaten by larger animals.

Say, for example, that chemicals were spilled in the environment. Plants might take them in. A mouse might eat lots of those plants, and store up the chemicals in them. An eagle or falcon might eat lots of mice, and store up so many chemicals that they cause illness, or the birds can't hatch healthy young birds.

People have learned about the dangers of pollution, and many of the chemicals such as DDT that once harmed raptors are now banned, or not allowed. It's a good reminder that we need to be careful with any chemicals we use, too.

People have found an interesting way to help some endangered birds such as peregrine falcons. Hacking is placing hand-reared chicks in the wild. Here's how it works:

Biologists select healthy adult birds. Their eggs are incubated and hatched in a laboratory. When the young are three or four weeks old they're moved to hack sites, artificial rearing nests. People feed and watch them closely—but not too closely. They keep their distance, dropping food through a long tube and keeping human contact to a minimum.

When the young bird's wings are strong enough for them to fly, they're released. They return to the hack site to eat, until they're wild enough to hunt on their own.

Helping endangered raptors sometimes means people need to make sacrifices. We visited Maine's Acadia National Park one summer, and saw a sign saying that a popular mountain-hiking trail was closed. We looked closer, and learned that peregrine falcons were nesting on the side of this mountain. That's why no people were allowed. We chose another trail, and were glad to know that flying above us might be one of the speedy falcons.

The hacking program has worked in some unusual places, too. In Detroit and several other large cities, biologists have released peregrine falcons, and have found them building nests and raising young high above the city on window ledges of tall buildings. The falcons quickly found that pigeons, so common in city parks, make fine dining indeed.

Great horned owl.

Other raptors fill important jobs in the wild, just like the peregrine falcons and bald eagles do. In the West, golden eagles and all kinds of hawks patrol the skies, keeping populations of other animals such as prairie dogs in balance. Across North America, owls slip through the night air on almost silent wings, killing and eating mice and other rodents.

Without these birds of prey, other animals would become too numerous for their own good. Some small creatures would really become pests to farmers and other people, and disease could spread.

It's thrilling to see raptors do their work, too. We'll always remember the canoe trip during which an osprey, also called the "fish hawk," dove from the sky into the river, emerging with a big trout.

People would be much poorer if they never saw raptors in flight.

Above: Osprey.
Opposite page: Golden eagle.

CHAPTER 11
Preserving
the Bird Watching Experience

Many of the things we see when bird watching stay with us forever. Sometimes it helps a lot, though, to do things that "preserve" our bird watching fun.

Many people who love to watch birds keep a list of all the birds they see. Some keep a list for each year, and another list of all the birds they've ever seen in their lives. That way they can use the yearly lists to compare this year's watching to last year's, and use the life list to tell when they've seen a bird they've never seen before. Maybe you can find someone who'll let you look at their yearly or life list.

Bird watching stores and clubs sometimes sell forms you can use for jotting down your yearly and life lists. But you can easily make your own, using a little notebook. Write down what you saw, where and when you saw it, and anything unusual about it.

Years from now, when you're trying to remember just where you saw that osprey diving for a trout, or when that first hummingbird came to your feeder, you can look back in your list or bird watching journal to refresh your memory.

Photographs are another way to preserve the fun of bird watching. You should know, though, that birds always look farther away in pictures than they did when you saw them. People who take a lot of bird pictures usually use special lenses called telephoto lenses.

Telephoto lenses are like telescopes, and make birds in pictures look closer and bigger than they would otherwise. Almost all the bird pictures you've ever seen were taken with telephoto lenses.

No matter what kind of camera and equipment you use to photograph birds, you'll almost surely get better pictures if you use a blind to keep the birds from seeing you. Get close to the food or water you've put out for the birds, stay as still as you can, and be ready to snap the picture when the bird comes. Patience is the thing bird photographers need most.

Opposite page: Florida Scrub jay.

You don't need fancy equipment to draw pictures of the birds you see. All you need is a pencil and paper. Colored pencils or markers do make it easier to get good drawings of the birds. But you can just write the name of the color in the area it belongs, if you want, and color it later.

Drawing birds is hard, because they move a lot. It's hard to get close to them, too. That's one reason mourning doves are among our favorite birds. They don't seem to mind people nearby.

A good way to start drawing birds is by studying mounted birds or photos. That helps you get used to drawing the shape of different bird parts. Then you're ready for the real thing. One good trick is to scribble the shape of the bird as fast as you can. Then, after the bird leaves or when you're done scribbling, you can erase some parts and make them look better.

You can write down the colors of the various parts. Or, if you know which bird it is, you can use a bird book later to color it in.

The best way to preserve your bird watching? Take notes about the birds you see and where you saw them. Take photographs, too. Then, add drawings to your notes. Those records, with the memories you carry inside you, will be things that make bird watching even more special for you.

To Learn More About Birds...

Many good books and tapes can help you learn more about bird watching and birds. Here are a few we really like. Your librarian can help you find more.

BOOKS

Harrison, Kit and Harrison, George. *America's Favorite Backyard Birds*. Simon and Schuster, New York, 1983.

Peterson, Roger Tory. *Peterson First Guide to the Birds of North America*. Houghton Mifflin Company, Boston, 1986.

Peterson, Roger Tory. *A Field Guide to the Birds: Eastern and Central North America*. Houghton Mifflin Company, Boston, 1980.

Robbins, Chandler S.; Bruun, Bertel; and Zim, Herbert S. *Birds of North America: A Guide to Field Identification*. Golden Press, New York, 1983.

Stokes, Donald. (various volumes). *A Guide to Bird Behavior*. Little, Brown and Company, Boston.

TAPES

Walton, Richard K. and Lawson, Robert W. *Backyard Bird Song*. (tape recording and booklet) (Peterson Field Guides). Houghton Mifflin Company, Boston, 1991.

Opposite page: Canada goose.

My Bird Watching Log

There's a special way to preserve the fun of bird watching, even if you never take a picture or sketch a bird. Write about it—either a few facts in a journal to remind you later, or a whole story.

A log is like a diary or a journal. It's a place where you can write down the names of the birds you see and the things you see happen while you're bird watching. When you run out of pages in this book, you can make another log in a notebook.

A bird watching log can help you. If you enjoyed bird watching at a certain place, or saw a certain bird there, you might want to go back again. Best of all, a bird watching log helps you remember your very own bird watching adventures.

Opposite page: Cowbird and Veery thrush eggs in thrush nest.

My Bird Watching Log

The date I went bird watching was _____

Here are the people I bird watched with _____
_____

Here's where I bird watched _____

Here's what the weather was like _____

Here's what the area looked like _____
_____

Here are the birds I saw _____
_____
_____

Here are the field marks of one of the birds (maybe one I hadn't seen before)_____
_____

Here's the most interesting non-bird thing I saw _____
_____

This bird watching trip was ___ great ___ good ___ okay ___ not too good

My Bird Watching Log

The date I went bird watching was _____

Here are the people I bird watched with _____
_____

Here's where I bird watched _____

Here's what the weather was like _____

Here's what the area looked like _____
_____

Here are the birds I saw _____
_____
_____

Here are the field marks of one of the birds (maybe one I hadn't seen before)_____
_____

Here's the most interesting non-bird thing I saw _____
_____

This bird watching trip was ___ great ___ good ___ okay ___ not too good

My Bird Watching Log

The date I went bird watching was _____

Here are the people I bird watched with _____
_____

Here's where I bird watched _____

Here's what the weather was like _____

Here's what the area looked like _____
_____

Here are the birds I saw _____
_____
_____

Here are the field marks of one of the birds (maybe one I hadn't seen before)_____
_____

Here's the most interesting non-bird thing I saw _____
_____

This bird watching trip was ___ great ___ good ___ okay ___ not too good

My Bird Watching Log

The date I went bird watching was _____

Here are the people I bird watched with _____
_____

Here's where I bird watched _____

Here's what the weather was like _____

Here's what the area looked like _____
_____

Here are the birds I saw _____
_____
_____

Here are the field marks of one of the birds (maybe one I hadn't seen before)_____
_____

Here's the most interesting non-bird thing I saw _____
_____

This bird watching trip was ___ great ___ good ___ okay ___ not too good

My Bird Watching Log

The date I went bird watching was _____

Here are the people I bird watched with _____
_____

Here's where I bird watched _____

Here's what the weather was like _____

Here's what the area looked like _____
_____

Here are the birds I saw _____
_____
_____

Here are the field marks of one of the birds (maybe one I hadn't seen before)_____
_____

Here's the most interesting non-bird thing I saw _____
_____

This bird watching trip was ___ great ___ good ___ okay ___ not too good

My Bird Watching Log

The date I went bird watching was _____

Here are the people I bird watched with _____
_____

Here's where I bird watched _____

Here's what the weather was like _____

Here's what the area looked like _____
_____

Here are the birds I saw _____
_____
_____

Here are the field marks of one of the birds (maybe one I hadn't seen before)_____
_____

Here's the most interesting non-bird thing I saw _____
_____

This bird watching trip was ___ great ___ good ___ okay ___ not too good

My Bird Watching Log

The date I went bird watching was _____

Here are the people I bird watched with _____
_____

Here's where I bird watched _____

Here's what the weather was like _____

Here's what the area looked like _____
_____

Here are the birds I saw _____
_____
_____

Here are the field marks of one of the birds (maybe one I hadn't seen before)_____
_____

Here's the most interesting non-bird thing I saw _____
_____

This bird watching trip was ___ great ___ good ___ okay ___ not too good

My Bird Watching Log

The date I went bird watching was _____

Here are the people I bird watched with _____
_____

Here's where I bird watched _____

Here's what the weather was like _____

Here's what the area looked like _____
_____

Here are the birds I saw _____
_____
_____

Here are the field marks of one of the birds (maybe one I hadn't seen before)_____
_____

Here's the most interesting non-bird thing I saw _____
_____

This bird watching trip was ___ great ___ good ___ okay ___ not too good

Index